Start Right Reader

GRADE 1 • BOOK 3

Printed in the U.S.A.

ISBN 978-1-328-70200-5

12 0877 26 25 24 23

4500863693 B C D E F G

MODULE 5

Contents

MODULE 6

Week 1

Week 2

Week 3

Get Started

Meet Miss Tan and her class. They are planning a skit. What will their skit be about? What jobs will the kids have? Read to find out!

Red Hen Skit

by Ivy Akana
illustrated by Sachiko Yoshikawa

"Class!" Miss Tan claps. "Hush, class. Come sit." Kids sit around Miss Tan on the big, thick rug. "We worked on **Red Hen.** We will make it a skit. We can call it **Red Hen,**" Miss Tan tells them.

"It will be lots of fun, but it will be lots of work as well," Miss Tan tells them. "Let us get on with it. Meg and Cal will plan the plot. When they get it as good as it can get, it will be our **Red Hen** skit."

"Ann will play Red Hen," said Miss Tan. "Glen is Dog."

"Flap! Flap! Cluck, cluck, cluck," Ann clucks like Red Hen.

"Yes! Yip, yip!" yaps Glen. Glen is glad that he is Dog. "Yip, yip!"

"Nell is Cat," Miss Tan went on.

"Not I!" yips Nell.

"Do not yip it like that," Ann tells Nell. "Can you hiss it, Nell?"

"Yes, I can hiss it, Ann," hisses Nell.

"Hiss!" Nell is glad that she is Cat.

Kids in class will do other fun jobs for **Red Hen.** Miss Tan will get them set up. Ron and Liz will plan the sets. Then Ron, Liz, and kids in class will make flat sets that can stack. Miss Tan will check them.

Kids in class will make passes for **Red Hen.** People will come to see it. Moms, dads, and kids will see **Red Hen.** Nell, Ann, and Glen will stun them with clucks, yips, and hisses. **Red Hen** will be a big hit!

Rhyming Word Hunt

Find the word in the story that fits each clue. Write the word.

1. This word rhymes with **man.**
   It is a first step in big projects.

2. This word rhymes with **map.**
   You use your hands to do it.

3. This word rhymes with **then.**
   It names a character.

Blend and Read

1.	clap	black	click	flap	block
2.	fluff	plum	cliff	glass	flip
3.	chin	chat	thin	that	path
4.	flick	plate	cloth	clad	flame

5. Ann can cluck like a hen.

6. Meg and Cal plan the plot.

Bags, Blocks, and Rugs

by Ivy Akana
illustrated by Sachiko Yoshikawa

Miss Tan has big tan bags for Red Hen, Cat, and Dog. "Ann! Glen! Nell!" Miss Tan calls.

Miss Tan clips the bags.

Ann slips on a bag. "I will make it red like Red Hen," said Ann.

Ann gets started on her bag. She dabs red on it. She sticks on bits of red cloth. It is Red Hen!

Nell works on her bag. She sticks fluff on it. Fluff sticks on Nell, too. Nell will make it work.

Glen gets to work on his bag. Glen puts black blobs on the back of his bag. Dog will have big black spots on his back.

Then Glen cuts two flaps and sticks them on his glasses.

Miss Tan has boxes for Ron and Liz. Miss Tan cuts slits in a big box. Ron will fix it up for Red Hen. Red Hen sits in it. Ann can fit in it.

Liz stacks blocks on top of a box.
The blocks set off the dog bed.
"Dog will sit on this bed," said Ron.
"Cat will nap on rugs that Ron found
in that black bin," adds Liz.

Ann dresses as Red Hen and gets in the big box. Glen dresses as Dog and sits on his dog bed. Nell dresses as Cat. She flops on the thick rugs and has a cat nap.
Miss Tan claps.

Picture Hunt

Which words name pictures in the last story?

blobs	cliff	clock	boxes
clams	flag	plot	glasses
blocks	fluff	flaps	plums

Make a list of pictures you find.
Can you find seven things?

Compare lists with a partner.
Did you find the same things?

Letter Mix-Up

Read the words below to a friend.

around	two	come	found
people	other	came	worked

Oh, no! The letters in the words got mixed up. Work with your friend. Put the letters in order to spell a word from the box.

1. c e m o
2. f d u o n
3. l e e o p p
4. a c m e
5. w t o
6. k o w d e r
7. h e t o r
8. r n a o u d

Skit Jobs

by Ivy Akana
illustrated by Sachiko Yoshikawa

"Have fun with this skit!" Miss Tan tells Meg and Cal.

"Jazz up the plot. Will Red Hen get mad at Cat and Dog? Will Red Hen be sad?"

Meg and Cal worked on the plot.

"Red Hen found big plums," Cal tells Meg. "Then Red Hen had plum jam." "But, Cal," Meg tells him, "Red Hen has to get Cat and Dog to say **Not I.** Let her beg them to pick plums."

"Yes, Meg, that is it!" said Cal.
"Let me jot that down. Red Hen begs Cat and Dog to pick plums, but Cat and Dog will not pick plums with Red Hen."
"Red Hen is sad," adds Meg.

Kids in class work on passes to **Red Hen.** Kids write **Red Hen** on passes. Other kids stick hens, cats, and dogs on them. Kids stack the **Red Hen** passes and slip them in bags.

When the **Red Hen** skit is as good as it can get, the class will sit around Cal and Meg on the rug. Cal and Meg will catch them up on the plot. Kids in class like **Red Hen** with plums and jam.

When Cal and Meg tell about **Red Hen,** Miss Tan claps. "Let us clap for them, class! This skit rocks!" Miss Tan tells them. "The passes and sets rock. I am glad that **Red Hen** will be such fun."

READ TOGETHER

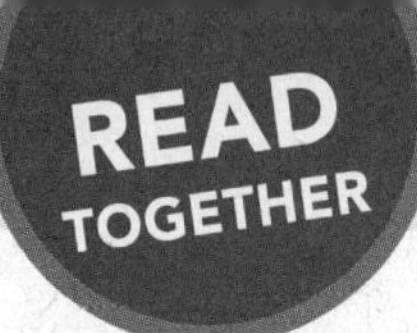

Story Events

Use the pictures to tell a friend about what has happened so far.

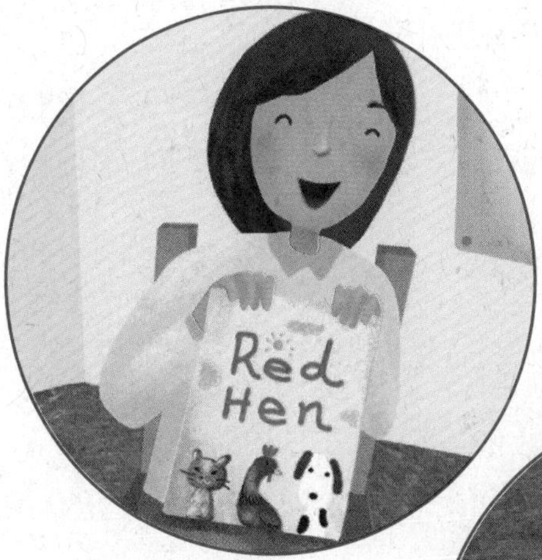

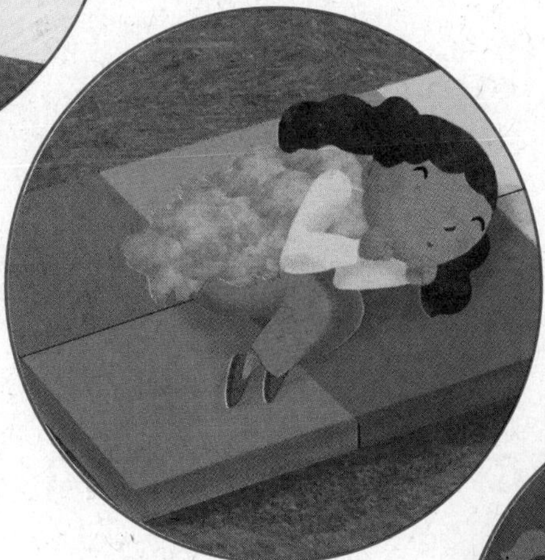

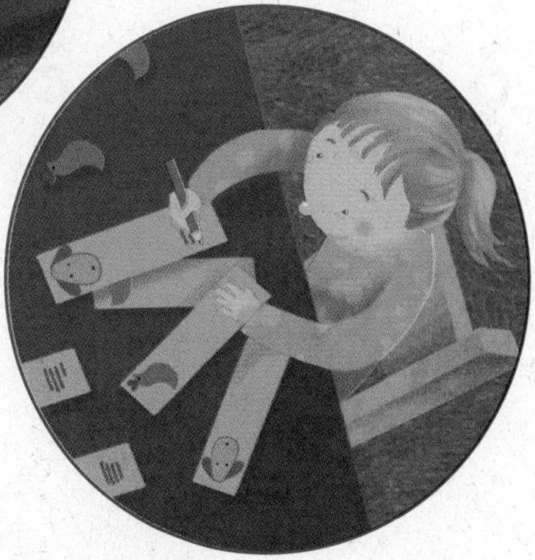

What do you think will happen next? Share your ideas with your friend.

Blend and Read

1.	clam	click	flash	flock	plot
2.	stop	slip	flop	clip	step
3.	well	wish	fill	dish	fell
4.	flesh	slab	blob	flick	blog

5. Kids make passes for **Red Hen.**

6. The kids clap for Meg and Cal.

Skit Day

by Ivy Akana

illustrated by Sachiko Yoshikawa

It is skit day! Moms and dads step in with passes for **Red Hen.** Miss Tan chats with them. Kids stack passes in a box.

Two classes come in. The kids sit on a big rug.

"I am glad you came," Miss Tan tells them. "This skit is **Red Hen.** This class did such good work on it. The kids did their jobs with skill. Let us clap for them."

Moms, dads, and kids clap.

Before **Red Hen** starts, Glen yells "My flaps came off!" but Liz has them. Glen sticks them back on his glasses. Glen is glad.

Glen is Dog. Ann is Red Hen. Nell is Cat. Liz checks the set.

Red Hen sat in her big box. Dog sat up in his block bed. Cat got up on the thick rugs. A hush fell.

Miss Tan nods. **Red Hen** starts.

"Plums! Big plums!" clucks Ann.

"Who will pick big plums with me?"

"Not I!" yips Glen.
"Not I!" hisses Nell.
"Cluck, cluck! Who will make plum jam with me?" Ann clucks.
"Not I!" yips Glen.
"Not I!" hisses Nell.

Red Hen is still quick to let them have plum jam. Red Hen tells Cat and Dog that she likes them.

"Let us pick plums with Red Hen, Dog!" said Cat. People clap.

Click! Flash! **Red Hen** is a big hit!

Turn and Talk

Reread the four stories. Then talk with a partner to answer these questions.

1. Make a list of the jobs that the kids do to put on the skit.
2. Which job for the skit is the hardest? Which is the easiest? Why do you think so?
3. Which job for the skit would **you** like to do? Why?

Get Started

What is fall like where you live? Is it cold? Do you see red on the trees or not?

What do animals do when fall is cold? What do people do? Read to find out about fall!

© Miao Liao/Shutterstock

Red, Red, Red

by Jillian Nash

It is fall when you can see stems
that are full of red, red, red!
All that red drops down on the grass.
It makes big red patches like thick
red rugs.
Fall is pretty. It is cold as well.

Ducks fly away in fall. Big flocks of ducks flap off to where it is not cold. Ducks quack as they flap. Ducks stop on this big trip to snack, chat, sip, plan, and nap. Then the ducks will flap, flap, flap away again.

Frogs hop less when it is cold. In fall, they nap in gaps in logs. Frogs can find such gaps in big logs.

Some bugs nap in cracks. Fat, wet slugs nap as well. You can spot them if you pick up rocks.

Bats can zip and grab bugs, but bugs can not fly well when it is cold. Bats nap then, because if bugs do not fly, bats can not get them. Bats can nap in thin cracks. Bats nap in big dens in cliffs as well.

What is this? It snacks on nuts. It snaps up bugs. It digs up grubs. It rips up big logs to find bits that it can eat. This one gets fat! Then it will nap in a big, dim den. It will live off its thick fat as it naps.

What can kids do when it is fall? Kids can make big red hills, toss them, and flop in them! Kids can hop in them or dig in them. Kids can drop and kick them. Kids can stuff them in big bags as well. Fun!

Word Clues

Use the clues to find words in the text. Write the words.

1. They hop less in the fall. They can nap in gaps in logs. What is the word?

2. Ducks take a big one of these in the fall. They fly to where it is not cold. What is the word?

Blend and Read

1. grab drag grip brag drip
2. frog prop trim drum truck
3. ditch stick fetch speck stack
4. grassy tricky frilly crabby dressy
5. Flocks of ducks fly away in fall.
6. Frogs and bugs nap in cracks.

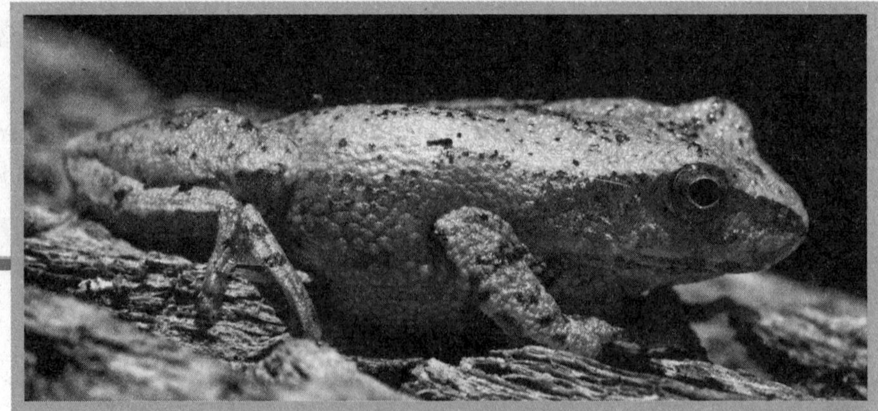

Big Crops

by Jillian Nash

Fall is rich with big crops. People can pick them. This big crop is red. Can you tell what it is? It is a big job to pick this crop.

The crop can go in big bins. The bins fill up!

People fill the big bins up to their brims. Then they stack full bins on big trucks. Lots of bins can fit on big trucks! Then the full trucks take the bins away.

Trucks get crops to shops as well. This man gets boxes off big trucks. He picks them up and lugs them to shops. Then his truck will zip to other shops to drop off big boxes.

Big stacks of this red crop make big red hills in shops. Other crops fill shops, too. What big crops can people get in this shop?

This mom makes rich snacks with fall crops. Mom chops them. Then she drops them in pans. Fill them up, Mom! Then pop them in and let them get hot. Yum, yum, yum! Fun snacks!

Can you tell what this big crop is? You can pick it in this patch. Cut the stem. Then pick it up, hug it, and lug it off. It is big! Kids can run in this big patch as well.

Fall wins! It is so much fun!

Read It, Change It

Read each word from the text. Then follow the directions to write a new word. Read each new word.

1. **drop** Change **d** to **c**.
2. **brim** Change **b** to **t**.
3. **truck** Change **u** to **a**.
4. **crops** Change **r** to **h**.

Check your work with a partner. Take turns using the new words in sentences.

Story Break

Read this text with a partner.

Ducks fly **away** from the **cold.** Frogs and bugs nap in cracks **or** gaps. It is **fall again.**

People pick crops. The boxes and bins are **full.** It is **pretty** all around **because** it is **fall again.**

Work with a partner. Add your own sentence to tell about fall.

Fetch, Dash, Dig

by Jillian Nash

Fall is when I fetch nuts. I am quick! I grab them, then run off with them. I pick up as much as I can. Others pick up nuts as well.

I dig pits. Plop, plop, plop! I drop nuts in them. Then pat, pat, pat! I tuck the nuts in them. It is such a big job!

I fetch nuts, dash, and dig. Then I fetch nuts, dash, and dig again!

I stash nuts because it will get cold. That is bad. Then I cannot get bugs, eggs, grubs, buds, or fresh nuts, but I can dig up nuts that I hid.

Shall I dig pits in this spot or there? This big patch is it!

Then big Red Fox pops up in the grass! That is bad! Big Red Fox is not my pal. I run, run, run and then trick Red Fox. I sit still. Red Fox can smell but not catch me. Red Fox is upset and will trot off uphill.

I will snack on nuts. I grip them, then nip them to crack their thick tan shells. As I nip, snip, chip at a big shell, it cracks!
Nuts! Yum, yum!

I fetch nuts, dash, dig, then hop in bed at sunset. Then I will fetch nuts, dash, and dig when I get up again. Fetch nuts, dash, dig, that is my plan! It is such a big, big job!

K-W-L Chart

Make a chart like the one below to show what you have learned about fall.

Fall		
K	**W**	**L**
What I **K**now	What I **W**ant to Know	What I **L**earned

Talk about your work in a group.

Blend and Read

1. into pickup cannot bathmat
2. upset lipstick flapjack checkup
3. paths batches cracks stitches
4. forget sunshine cupcake playmate
5. The big red fox trots uphill.
6. See the pretty red sunset!

Red, Red Sunset

by Jillian Nash • illustrated by Lisk Feng

"Be quick, Fred!" calls Mom. "We can go see the sunset."

"Yes, Mom!" yells Fred. He fetches his red hat because it is cold. Mom grabs a black hat.

Fred runs to catch up with his mom. She gets in the big red pickup truck with black mud flaps.

"Hop in," Mom tells Fred. Then Mom starts the pickup truck.

Putt, putt, putt! The pickup truck chugs uphill. It is on a zigzag path. Mom and Fred pass ditches, cliffs, and rocks. Fred spots a bobcat on a big log.

Mom stops the pickup truck on the hilltop. Fred hops out and sits on a big flat rock.

Mom gets mats. "That rock is cold!" Mom tells Fred.

The sunset is pretty. It has red flashes. "Fred, get snapshots," Mom tells him.

Fred grins. Mom hugs Fred.

Click, click!

Mom claps. "Good shots, Fred!"

Then the sun sets. Fred picks up the mats. He gets back in the pickup truck. Mom hops in as well.

The pickup truck chugs back downhill.

"That sunset trip was fun," Fred tells Mom.

Think-Pair-Share

Reread the four texts. Think and then talk with your partner.

1. What is something you might see an animal do in the fall? Why?
2. What would **you** like to do in the fall? Why?

Share your ideas with a group.

Get Started

This is Cass. She will be starting to go to Class Six after school.

What is Class Six? What will Cass do there? Who will she meet? Read to find out!

Class Six

by Emma Redbird
illustrated by Paul Hoppe

It is the bell. Class is done. Kids got up and left their desks as they got their backpacks, class work, and lunch boxes and then went to their spots. A teacher will pick Cass up from class.

Many kids got on buses or left with moms and dads, but Cass did not go with them. Her mom is still at work. Cass has Class Six. This makes Cass a bit glum and upset.

"Kids have fun in Class Six," the teacher tells Cass. "Miss Bond makes grand plans and the kids help. It will be fun."

Cass steps into Class Six. Some kids sit, but others hop and jump.

"Miss Bond, this is Cass. Cass, this is Miss Bond," the teacher tells them. "Cass is in Class Six," he adds. Miss Bond grins at Cass. "It is Frog Day in Class Six, Cass. You can jump like a frog with the kids in Class Six."

Two kids hop up. "This is Fran," Miss Bond tells Cass, "and this is Ken. Fran and Ken will help you."

Cass cracks a grin at Fran and Ken. "What is Frog Day?" Cass asks. Fran and Ken just laugh and jump.

"Miss Bond plans the days for us in Class Six," Ken tells Cass. "Today is about frogs—and frogs hop!"

"Will you hop with us, Cass?" asks Fran. Then Cass and Fran and Ken hop with kids in Class Six.

What Is the Word?

Use the clues to find words in the story.

Clue 1: many kids like to do this
Clue 2: rhymes with **pump**
What is the word?

Clue 1: means **big** or **splendid**
Clue 2: rhymes with **hand**
What is the word?

Now you do it! Give two clues about a story word. Can a partner find the word?

Blend and Read

1.	lamp	last	best	help	damp
2.	send	rent	stand	bent	prompt
3.	mash	chip	batch	rich	much
4.	crisp	zest	drift	jest	clump

5. Miss Bond plans for Class Six.

6. Cass jumps with Fran and Ken.

Frogs in Class Six

by Emma Redbird

illustrated by Paul Hoppe

Miss Bond has the kids sit on the rug. Miss Bond tells them about frogs. "Frogs live in damp, wet spots. They swim and hop well. Frogs can take long rests in ponds or on land. Frogs catch bugs."

Then Miss Bond tells the kids that they will play a bit more. Miss Bond tells them about **Big Frog Pond.** Cass, Ken, and Fran hop to Big Frog Pond. It has logs, plants, and bags that look like bugs.

Cass tosses a bug bag. It lands on the first plant. Cass does not hop on that plant. She hops up and back. Then Cass stands on one leg. She bends and picks up her bug. Fran and Ken clap.

Fran tosses the next bug. She jumps, but then she lands on the plant with the bug. Fran must stop.

Then Ken tosses his bag and hops up and back. When Ken picks up his bug, he falls. Ken must stop.

The kids play again. Cass did not land on any plants with bugs.

"I think Cass hops and jumps the best. Cass picks up bugs well. Cass wins Best Frog! Cass wins Best Frog!" Fran chants.

Moms and dads pick up their kids.

"Will you come back to Class Six?" Ken asks Cass. "It is much more fun with you in it."

"Yes, Ken!" Cass grins and laughs. "I had lots of fun in Class Six!"

Rhyming Word Hunt

Find the word in the story that fits each clue. Write the word.

1. This word rhymes with **vests.** You sit still to do it.

2. This word rhymes with **ant.** It is usually green.

3. This word rhymes with **lands.** Cass does it on one leg.

Use That Word

Take turns. Play with a friend until you use all the words.

any	more	best	done	laugh
pull	long	think	just	teacher

1. Pick a word and read it.
2. Your friend uses the word in a sentence.
3. Then your friend picks a word and reads it.
4. You use your friend's word in a sentence.

Crafts in Class Six

by Emma Redbird
illustrated by Paul Hoppe

It is the bell. Class is done. Her mom has to work, but Cass is not glum any more. Cass has pals in Class Six, and Miss Bond is fun. Cass skips off to Class Six with the teacher who went with her before.

Fran and Ken pull Cass into Class Six.

"What did Miss Bond plan for us, Fran?" Cass asked.

"It is Craft Day, Cass!" Fran winked at Cass and added, "We kids think and plan, and then we make stuff."

"Miss Bond lets us pick any bits of stuff on this desk," Fran went on. "Get as much as you want, Cass." Fran got a long sock and stuck felt on it. Then Fran pulled it up on her hand. "It is my sock cat, Socks!"

Ken got a soft cloth sack and stamped spots on it. "Add more spots," Fran prompted him.

Ken did just that. Then he pulled the sack up on his hand. "Spot is a dog that can do tricks," said Ken.

Cass got a thin red box and added fins and gills. Then she slid sticks in the box and held it up with them.

"Is that a fish, Cass?" Fran asked.

"Yes," Cass said. "This is Flick. His fins flash in the sun."

Fran, Ken, and Cass think up a quick skit with Socks, Spot, and Flick. Ken, Cass, and Fran put it on for Miss Bond and Class Six. The kids laugh and clap when it is done. It is a big hit in Class Six!

READ TOGETHER

Characters

Think about the characters.

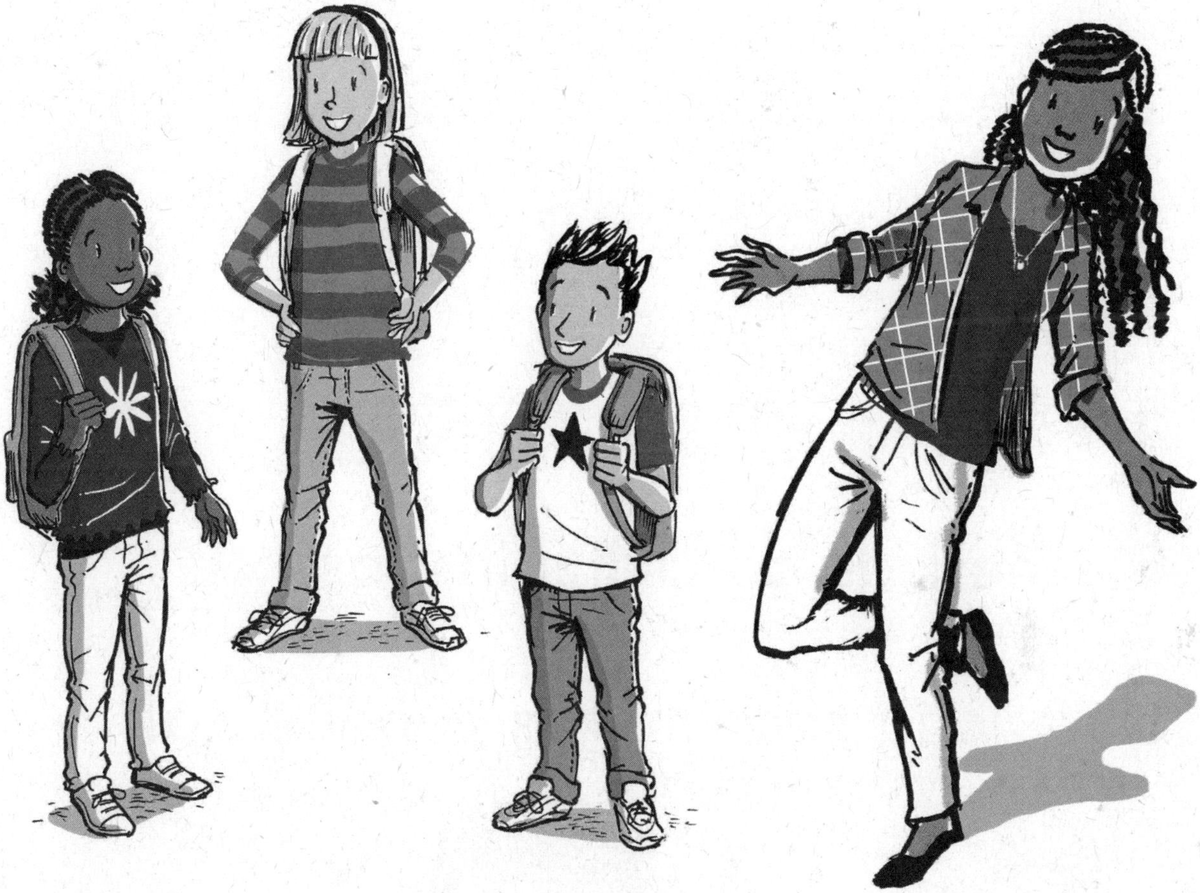

Write two things you learned about each character. Share your work with a partner.

Blend and Read

1. picked rested lasted packed
2. filled listed added prompted
3. dishes moths dresses hatches
4. brand cramp drifted ramps
5. The kids do crafts in class.
6. A long sock makes a good cat.

Track in Class Six

by Emma Redbird
illustrated by Paul Hoppe

"It is Track Day! Today you can run, toss, and jump," Miss Bond tells Class Six. "Stick with two pals," she tells the kids. "One pal will run, one will toss, and the last one will jump."

First, Fran and other Class Six kids will run. The kids run fast!

Cass and Ken jump up and down.

"Fran!" "Fran!" Cass and Ken yell for Fran. Who will win?

Fran wins! Fran is the champ!

Ken and Class Six kids will toss next. A long toss will win it. Ken and the kids toss. The last kid tosses! Will Ken win?

Ken tossed a good toss, but he did not win. The last kid is the champ.

Then Cass and Class Six kids will jump. "I think I can land this jump," Cass tells Fran and Ken.

"You can do it," Fran tells Cass.

"This is it, Cass! Get set to jump!"

Cass and the kids got set. Fran and Ken chanted, "Cass, Cass, Cass, Cass! Jump, Cass, jump!"

Cass ran fast and then jumped! Will Cass win? Cass jumped well, but she did not win. A big kid won.

"I am glad that I am in Class Six," Cass said. "It is the best, and our teacher is such a blast! What will Miss Bond plan next?" Fran and Ken just laughed and bumped fists. "I bet it will be fun!" said Cass.

Think-Write-Pair-Share

Reread the four stories. Think and then write answers to these questions.

1. How do Cass's feelings about Class Six change? How do you know?

2. What would **you** like best about Class Six? Why?

Share your work with a partner and then in a group.

Get Started

What do you know about houses? What can houses look like? What can be used to make them? Read to find out!

House

by Margaret Fetty

What is a house? It is where we live. We can rent or own a house.

What do we do in houses? We do a lot in them! We can eat, chat, and rest in them. We can ask pals over to say "hi!" and have fun with us!

What jobs can a house do? It can stop big gusts of wind. It can block the hot sun and cold winds. It can stop drips and drops. We will not get wet in it. It can shut out bugs and pests as well.

Who can be in houses? Moms, dads, and kids can. Best pals can. Grandpops and grandmoms can be in them. Pets can be in them.

Many can be in one house and not many in another. It is up to us.

We like to fix up houses and make them our own. We can add on to them. It is up to us. We do odd jobs in them. We pick up trash in them. We mop, dust, and pick up stuff so we don't trip over it.

A house can be a hut that is as little as a tent, or it can be as big as ten jets.

It can stand up on cliffs and hilltops. It can be dug into hills. It can sit next to water or rest on top of it. It is up to us.

People can make houses with stuff that is around us. We can make them with grass, plants, sticks, and logs.

We can make them with bricks, rocks, mud, and sand, or lots and lots of glass! It is up to us.

Word Clues

Find and write the words in **House** that answer each clue.

1. We use this word to say "hello."
2. This word means "for that reason."
3. **Is** and **are** are forms of this word.

Blend and Read

1.	be	hi	he	so	me
2.	go	she	we	no	do
3.	tuft	stilts	grid	drab	lash
4.	sod	notch	latch	lug	trot

5. Houses can be big or little.

6. We go to my house to eat.

Houses That Go Up

by Margaret Fetty

Look at this house! It stands up over water. Big logs lift it up so it will not get wet. The logs are stilts. It is a stilt house.

People get logs, grass, and sticks on land to make this house.

This is another house on stilts. It is in a hot, wet land that has lots of plants in it.

This house has thatch up on top. It slants so water runs off it. Pests like rats and frogs do not get into it.

This house is in another hot and wet land. Men cut notches in logs to help them grab onto the logs. Then they lug logs, sticks, and grass up and get it made.

It is just grand up at the top!

In the past, some people had big houses up on cliffs. Men cut rock into thick blocks and then stacked them. This gave them a way to see over hills and lands. It helped them fend off men with plans to rob them.

Kids can play in houses that are up on big sticks. It is fun! This one is so big that people can live in it.

It has beds and lamps. It has hot water and bathtubs. It has spots to chat and catch a sunset. It is fun!

We can go up, up, up in this big house! It is not one big house. It is like lots of houses on top of one another.

Lots of us can fit in it! It is fun to go up and down its steps.

Hunt for Words

1. Look in the text for words with long **e** and long **o**. Write each word you find.

2. Look at your list of words. Circle the word with the long **e** sound. Underline the words with the long **o** sound.

3. Write two words that rhyme with each set of words. Share your lists with a partner.

Sentence Starters

Learn these words. You will see them in your reading and use them in your writing. Read the words to a partner.

over	**gave**	**house**	**another**
own	**read**	**water**	**white**

Use the sentence starters to talk about your reading.

1. We **read** about lots of _____.
2. A **house over water** is _____.

Use other words in the box to tell about the texts.

Grass, Mud, Logs, and Sod

by Margaret Fetty

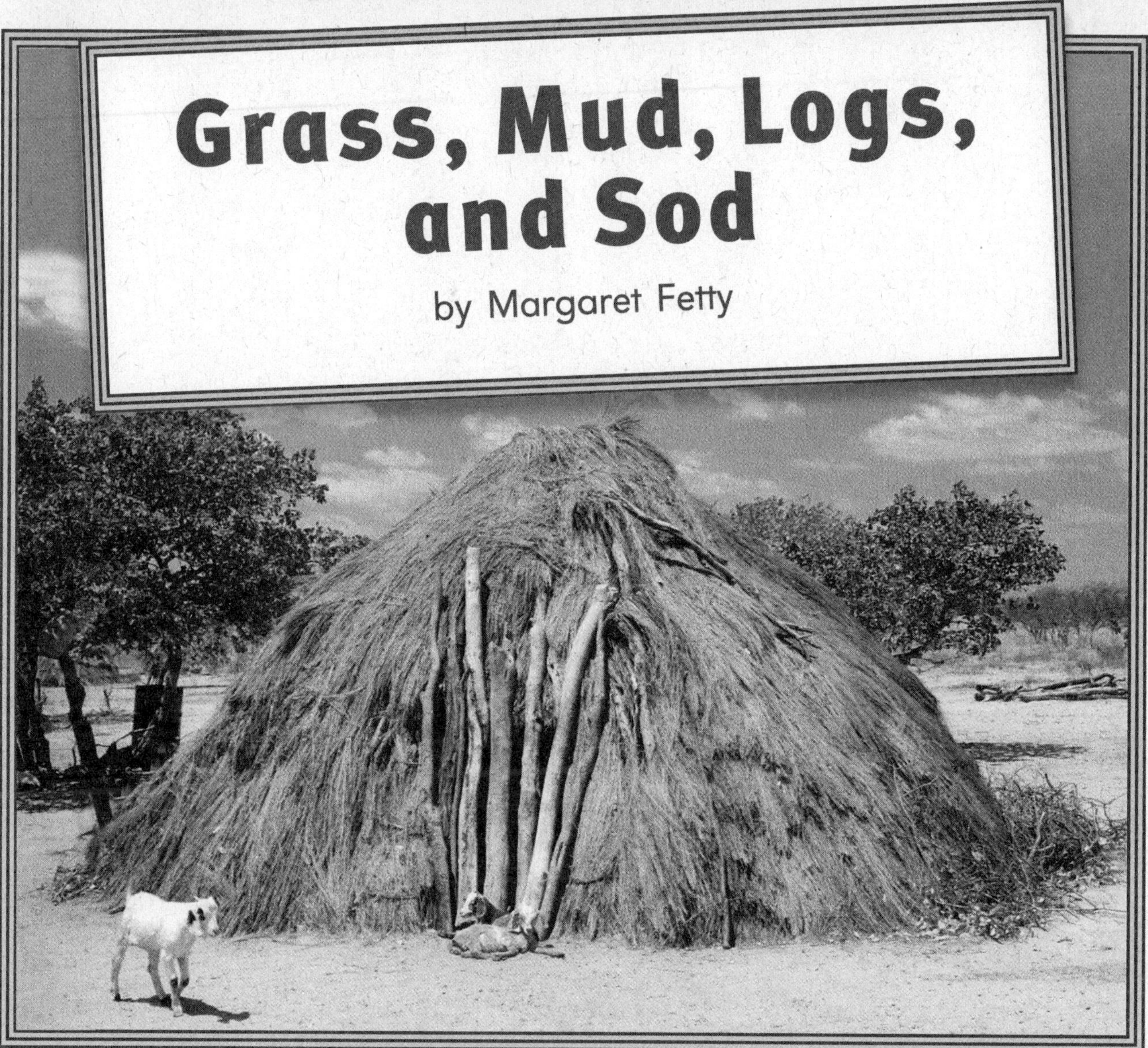

Houses can be made in many ways. Grass grows well in this hot land, so people make huts with it.

They pack sticks in grids and map out big boxes, tuck grass tufts over the sticks, and lash them up on top.

This land is hot, but not so wet. Big plants do not grow well, so people mix up mud, sand, and water and press them into bricks.

They stack the bricks, dab on a white mix, and add grass up on top.

This is another hot land that has houses made with mud bricks. People stack bricks and prop them with logs. Houses sit one next to another, blocked from sun and wind, so it is not hot in the houses.

© Sara Denlin/EyeEm/Getty Images

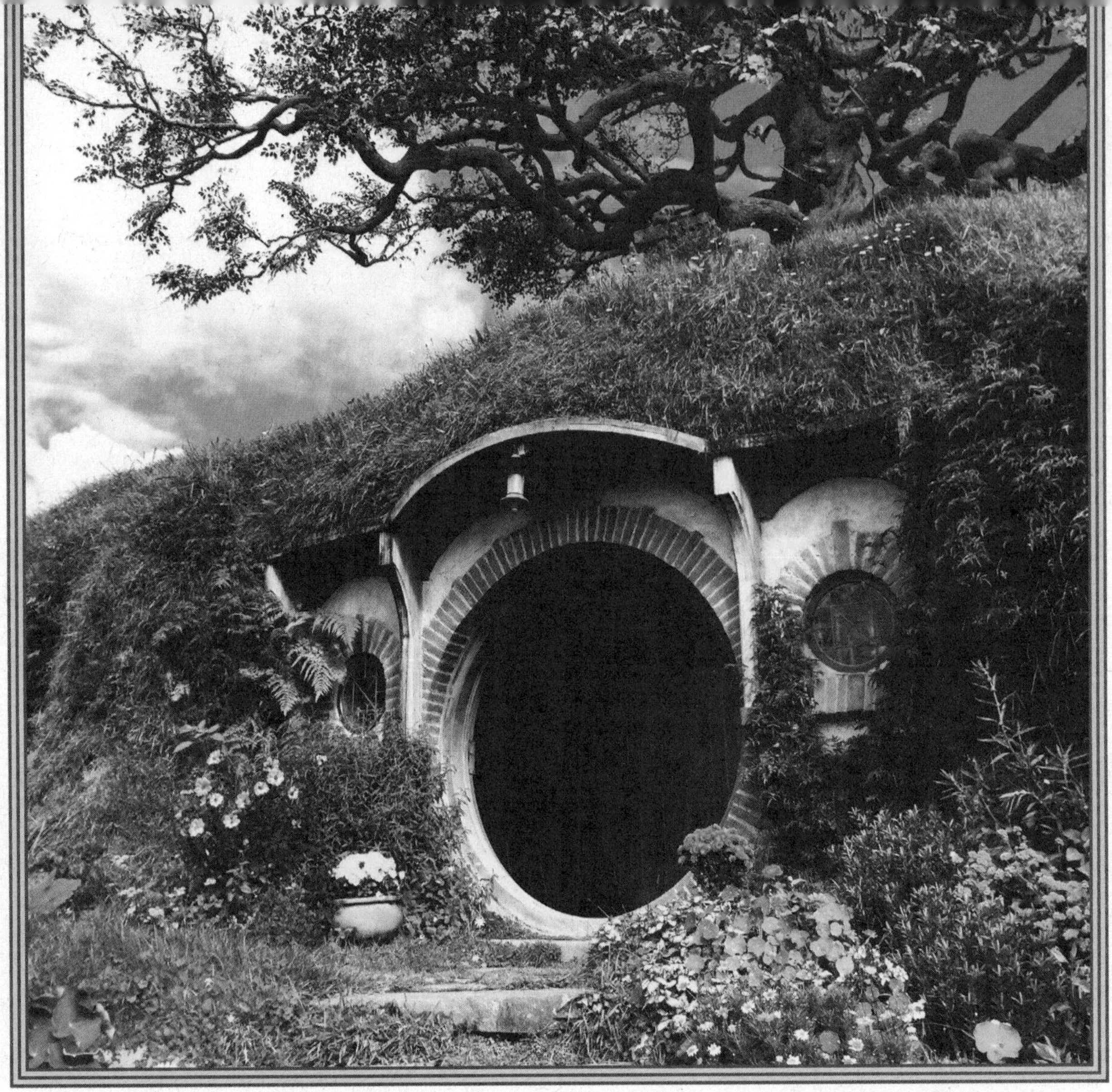

This house is in a hill. It has thick rock around it. Water cannot get into it. The hill helps it be snug.

Is it damp, black, and drab in this house? No, it is not! It lets in the sun, and it can be lit with lamps.

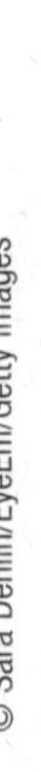

In the past, men cut logs and made log houses in which to live. Now we can get kits to set them up!

A man had logs sent with a kit to set up this log house. He read the plan. It gave tips to help him with it.

In the past, in lands with no logs, men cut sod into bricks and stacked them up to make sod houses.

Sod blocks got cut into big, thick bricks. Can you spot grass in this sod house's bricks?

Compare and Contrast

Write about two of the houses from your reading.

1. Tell two ways the houses are alike.
2. Then tell two ways the houses are different.

Share your work with a group.

Blend and Read

1. she hi so he mom's
2. dog's we no go be
3. sunset fact brim bathmat
4. logjam theft fend houseboat
5. This land's cliffs are so pretty!
6. We have read the kit's plans.

Houses That Can Go

by Margaret Fetty

Have you read of a spot that you wish to see for yourself? This tin house can help you with that wish.

You can go on trips with it. You can hitch it up to trucks and vans. Then off it goes—with you in it!

Another way to go to fresh spots is to camp in tents. It is fun and so pretty when you get there!

Tents fit in big backpacks. People put them on and go on paths that trucks and vans cannot go on. Zip up a tent's flap to block the wind.

People in this land tend flocks. As flocks go to get to grass, people go with them. They go with tents that are quick to set up and take down.

Sticks prop up one end. Mats and rugs block the sand and hot sun.

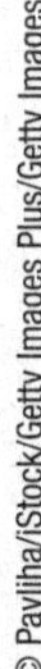

This tent is a big help in cold lands. White mats slip over thick sticks that prop them up. Rugs in the tent stop cold winds. It is snug in this tent. People can pack it up, get it on a yak, and be on their way.

This is a hot land. People tend flocks in this land and use huts that they can pack up fast. They make them with sticks and grass mats.

It is quick to pack them up and set off after a flock on the go.

Hi! This is my house. It cannot go on land, but it can go on water! It is so much fun to go on trips in it!

It has dishes, beds, rugs, and a bathtub. I mop and wax the deck. I do another job. Then I sit and rest!

Think-Draw-Pair-Share

Reread and think about the four texts. Then draw to answer these questions.

1. Which house do you think is the most interesting? Why?

2. How does one of the houses fit well with the land around it?

3. Which house would **you** like to live in? Why?

Share your work with a partner and then with a group.

READ TOGETHER

Get Started

Meet Kate, Dave, Liz, and Tuck. They like to go on trips together.

On this trip, they will go camping. What will they do? Will they have fun? Read to find out!

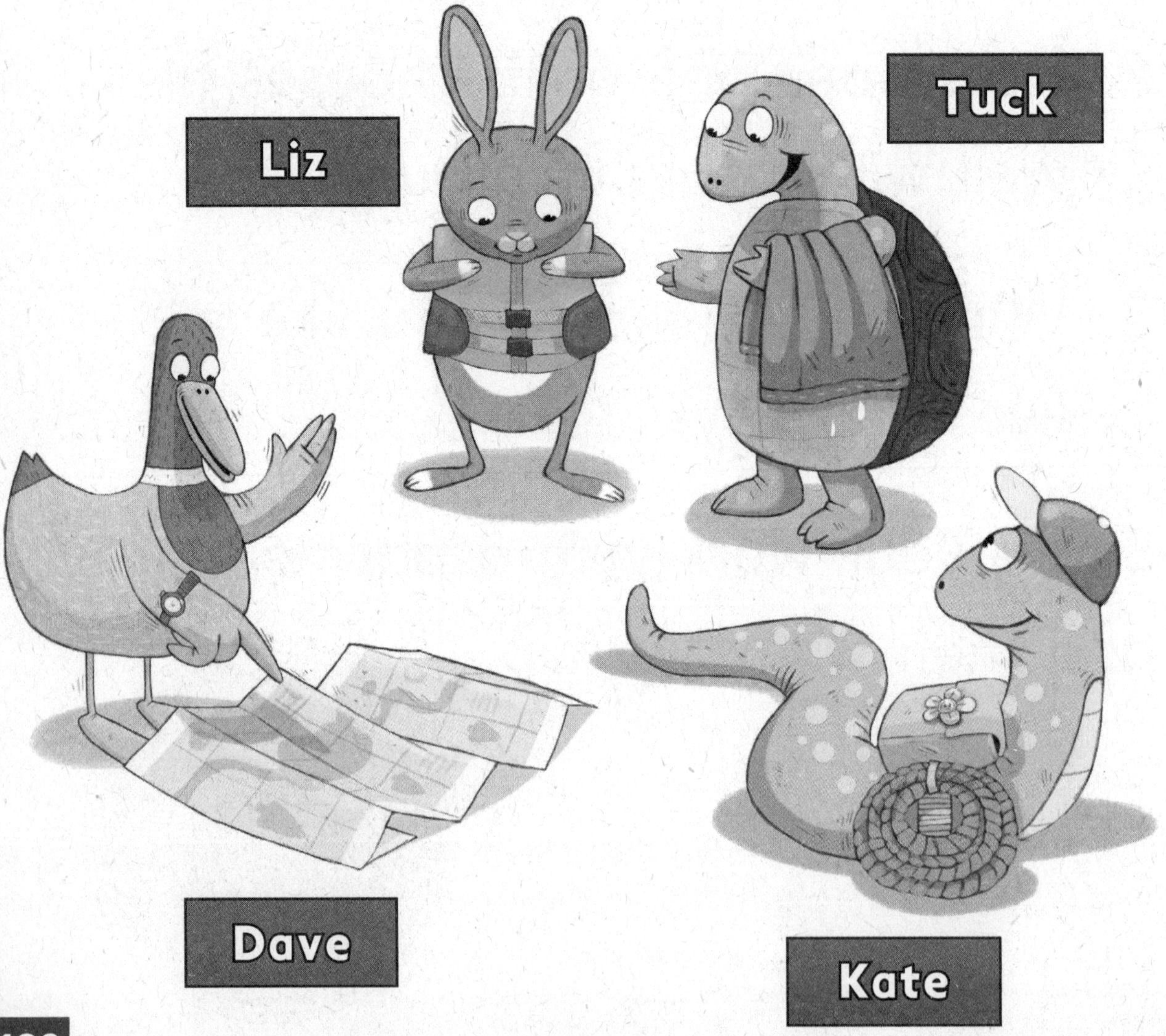
Liz
Tuck
Dave
Kate

Brave Kate

by Kippy Dalton • illustrated by Mary Sullivan

Kate, Dave, Liz, and Tuck are best pals. They always do fun things. The best pals play games, trade stuff, and plan trips to take.

On this trip, the pals will camp out at Crane Lake. It will be such fun!

"This is a good spot," Liz tells the others. "We should set up camp."

Kate gets the tent cloth on its rods. Liz stamps in tent stakes. Dave rubs sticks to make a flame. Tuck makes them hot things to eat.

The pals ate fish, eggs, and grits. They sat still and looked at the sunset. Then they all went to bed.

The tent puffed up and went flat.

"What is that?" asked Liz.

"It must be the wind," Kate said.

"What is that **swish, swish?"** asked Tuck. "It makes me upset."

"It is just the wind," said Kate. "It hits branches that hit the tent."

"Kate is brave," Tuck said, "but I am not. I tuck into my shell."

Thump, thump, thump! Dave began to shake. "What is that, Kate?" he asked. "It upsets me."

"Yes, what is that?" asked Liz. "It upsets Dave and Tuck—and me!"

"Shall I go check?" Kate asked.

Kate left the tent to go check things out. Kate is so brave!

When she comes back in, Kate tells them, "It is the wind! The wind shakes down nuts that thump on our tent." Kate gives her pals nuts.

Rhyming Word Hunt

Find the word in the story that fits each clue. Write the word.

1. This word rhymes with **same.** Dave makes it with sticks.

2. This word rhymes with **lakes.** Liz stamps these in for the tent.

3. This word rhymes with **bake.** Dave does this when he is upset.

Blend and Read

1.	cake	wade	wake	trade	brake
2.	shape	brave	tape	wave	cape
3.	stack	slick	pitch	patch	damp
4.	blade	scale	spade	tame	crate

5. Shall Dave make another flame?

6. Kate is a very brave snake.

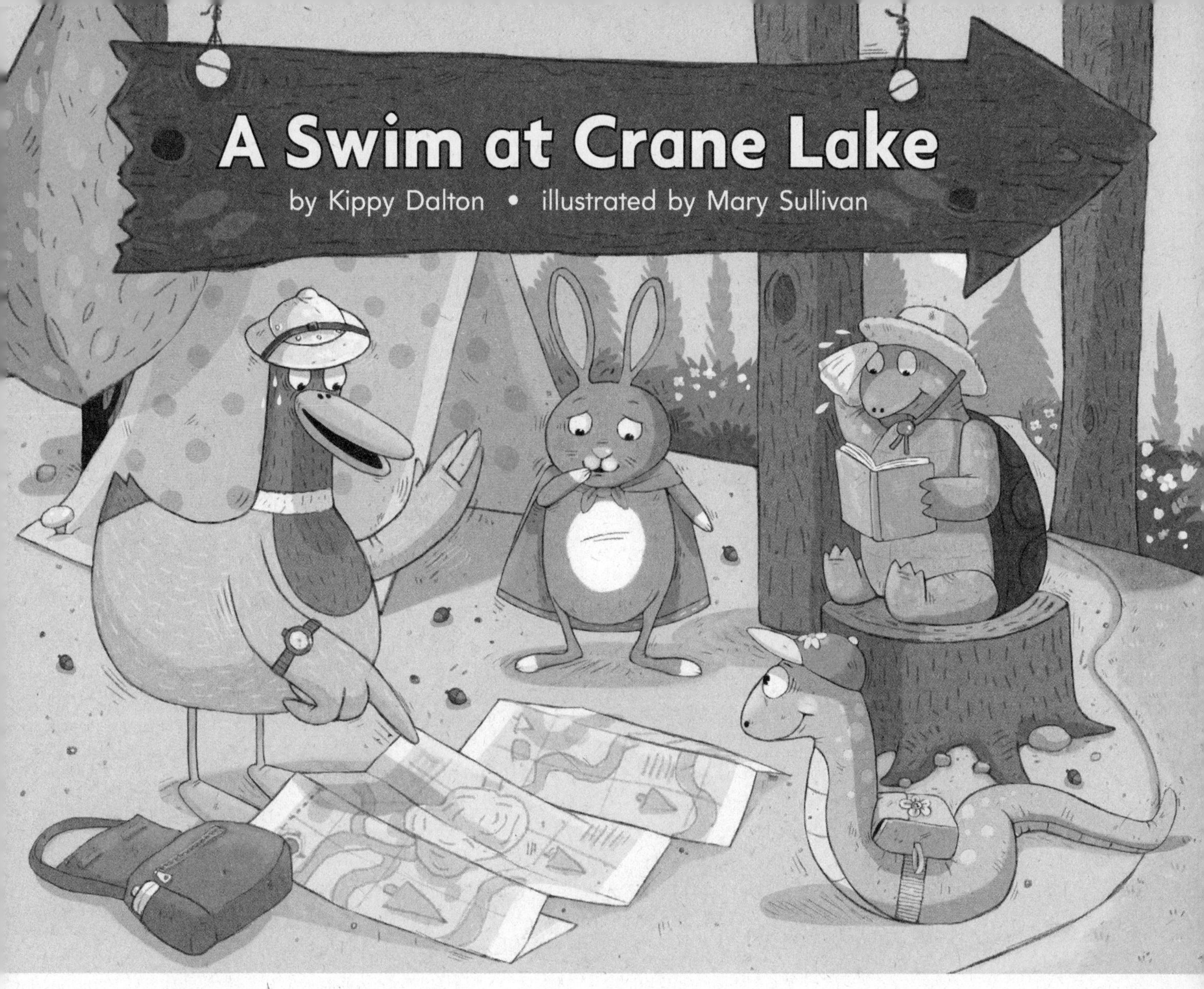

A Swim at Crane Lake

by Kippy Dalton • illustrated by Mary Sullivan

Dave takes out a map. "It is so hot! We should go for a swim. We can take a swim at Crane Lake."

Liz grins and nods. "That is not a bad plan, Dave. I do not swim well, but I can wade. It should be fun!"

The pals go on to Crane Lake. Dave and Kate swim. Tuck can swim, but he wades with Liz.

"What is that flat thing?" Liz asks.

"That is a raft," said Tuck. "Shall we take it out, Liz? It will be fun."

Liz and Tuck go to the dock. Tuck gives Liz a swim vest. "Use this vest," he tells her. "It will help if you end up in the lake."

Liz puts on the swim vest. She and Tuck get on the raft.

Dave and Kate swim to them and hop onto the raft. "I can see so many fish!" Liz tells them.

Kate and Dave bend to look.

"Look out!" Tuck yells as the raft rocks and tips them into the lake.

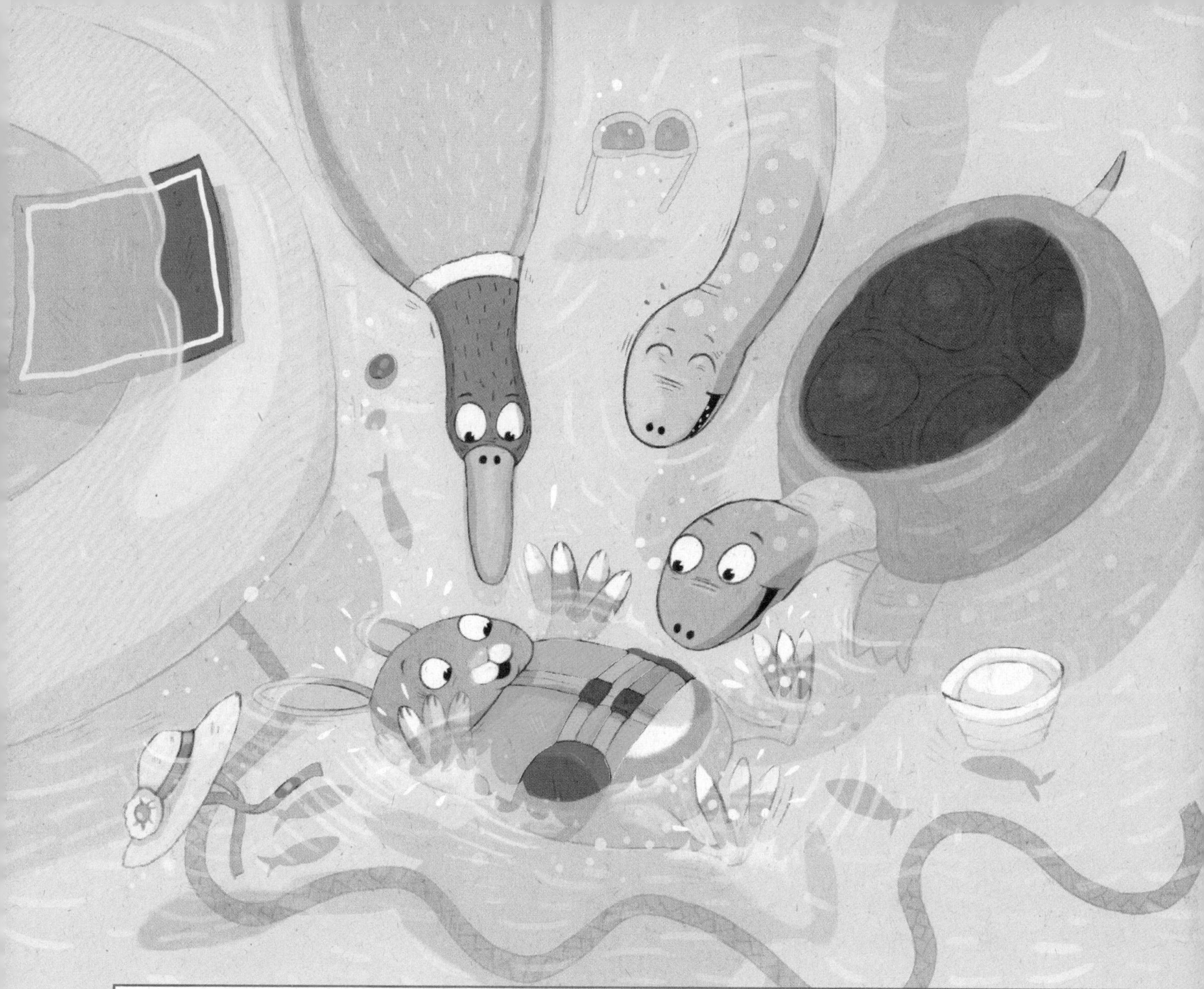

Up pop Dave, Kate, Tuck, and Liz. No one is hurt. Tuck began to laugh, and then Liz, Dave, and Kate laughed with him. Look at Liz!

"Tuck, this vest helped me, but I cannot swim like this," she tells him.

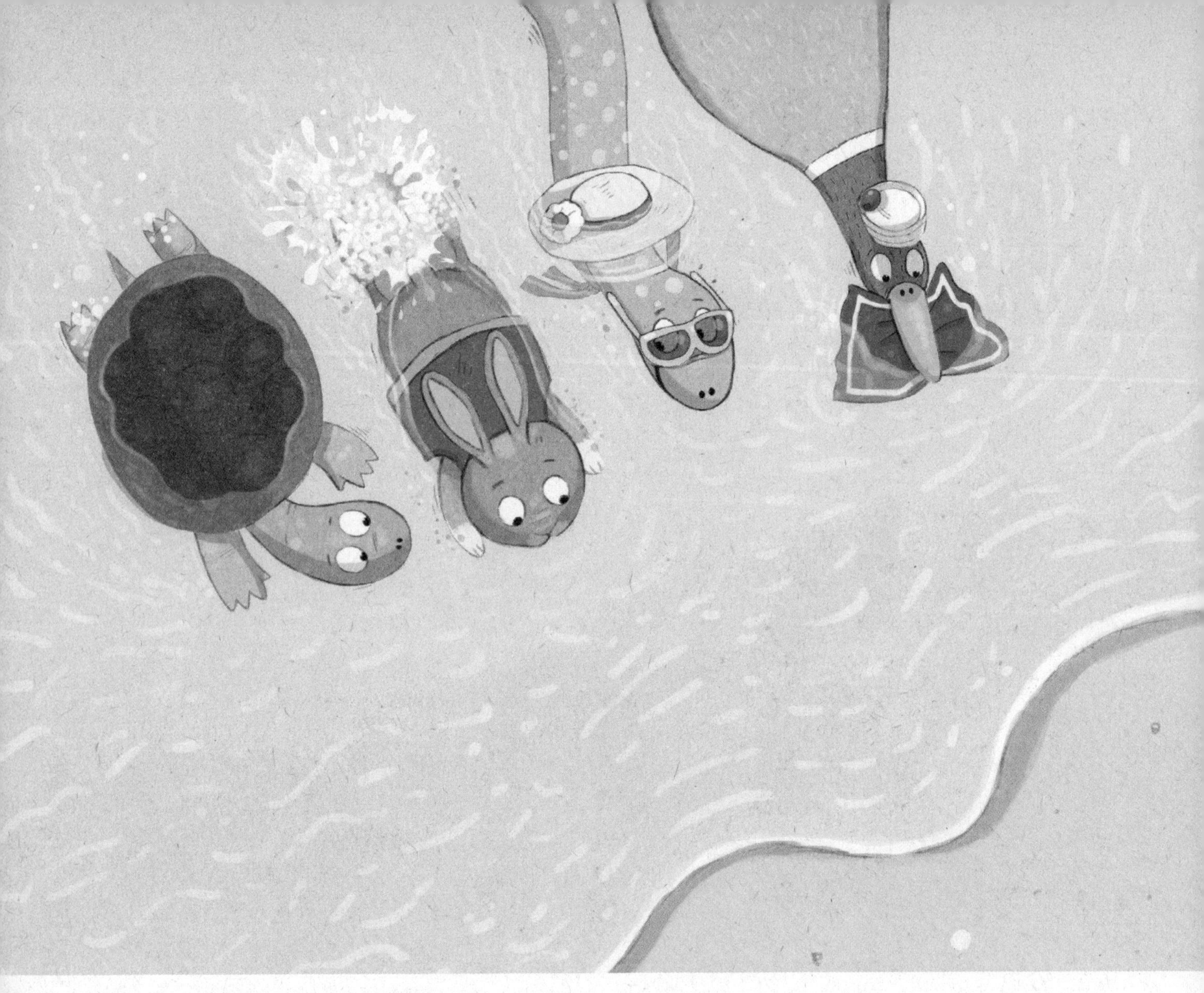

Tuck helped Liz get off her back. "This should be better, Liz," he said. "Kick! That is it! We will help you swim back. So, was it fun, Liz?"

"It was the best, but I will always take a swim vest if I go on a raft!"

Story Word Clues

Read the clues. Find the word in the story that answers each clue.

1. These two words tell what Dave does to the map. What does Dave do?

2. Liz cannot swim well, but she can do this. What is the word?

3. The raft tips the pals into this. What is the word?

Story Word Hunt

Read the words below to a partner.

began always hurt better gives

place should shall things gave

1. Together, look for each word in the last story. What words were not there?

2. Choose a word from the box. Write a sentence using the word. Read your sentence to your partner.

Race at the Skate Track

by Kippy Dalton • illustrated by Mary Sullivan

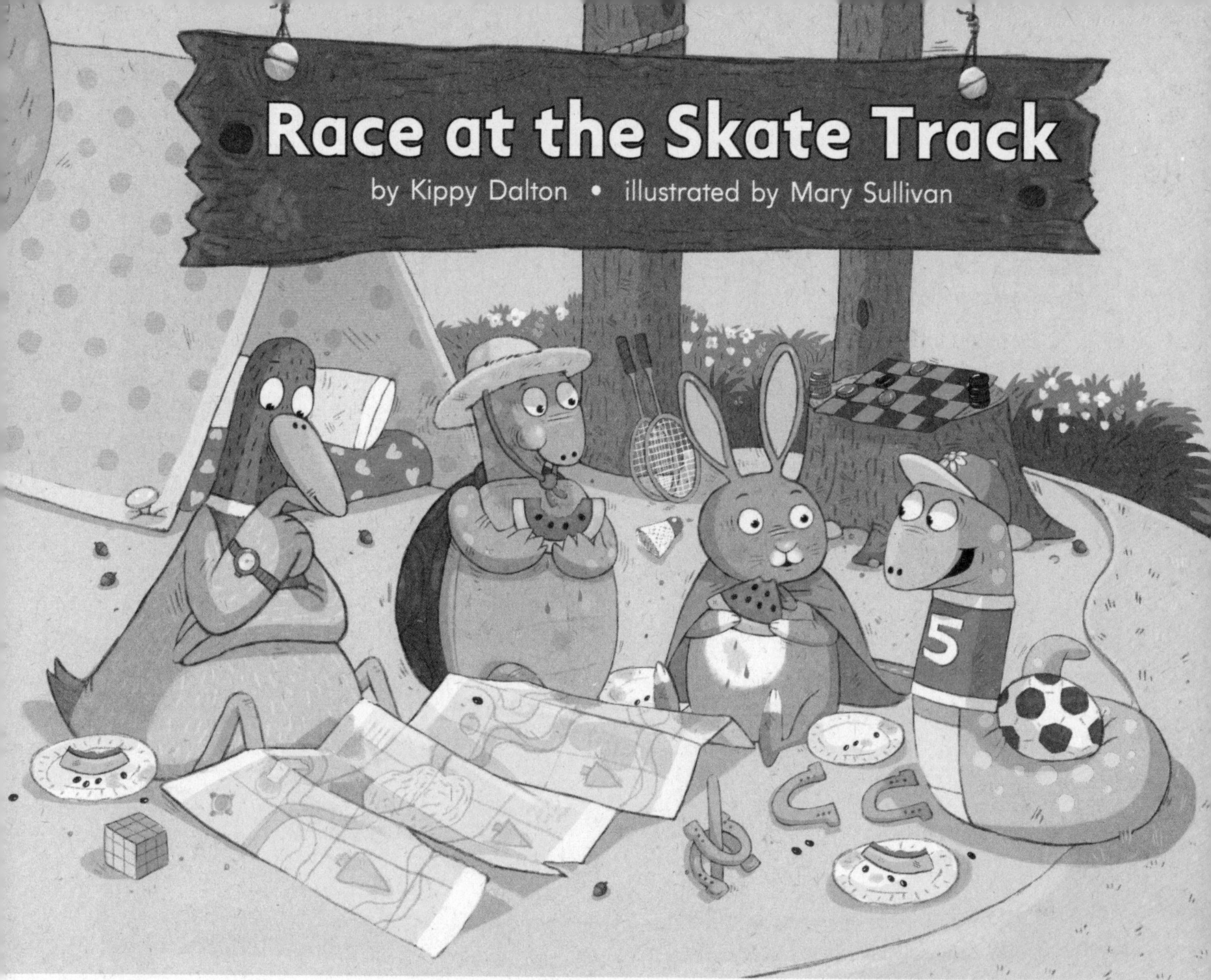

"What shall we do next?" Tuck asked his pals. "Should we race?"

"No," said Kate. "Liz runs better than we do. She will always win."

"We can go to the skate track," said Liz. "Then we can all skate."

The pals go to the skate track. It is the best place to skate! It rents skates for ten cents.

"Pads and other things help us be safe on skates," Liz tells them. "We should always be safe on skates."

Off went Dave, Tuck, and Kate.

"Not too fast!" Liz yelled, but Tuck fell and spun out. Tuck was not hurt, but he lost a skate.

"Come with me, Tuck! Hop on," Liz tells him.

Kate hit a bump with a big thump. She fell down on the track. Tuck asked if she was hurt.

"No, but this thing got a big crack in it," Kate tells him.

"Hop on, Kate!" Liz tells her.

Then Dave went off the track and fell down. Liz asked if he got hurt.

"No, I am not hurt, but I got mud in my skates," Dave said.

"Come with us," Liz tells Dave. "We can make space! Hop on!"

Liz began to go. She went fast, but not too fast. Dave, Tuck, and Kate held on as they went.

Tuck laughed. "That was fun!"

"We had a fast race with Liz," said Kate, "and we all win! Go, Liz!"

Setting

A story's setting is **where** and **when** it takes place. Think about the four stories. Then answer the questions.

1. How is the setting the same for all the stories?

2. In what ways does the setting change from story to story?

3. What is something **you** might like to do in a setting like this?

Talk about your answers in a group.

Blend and Read

1. face cent came space lace
2. cell race grace place trace
3. sick chase cave cluck much
4. nice price fine bike cone
5. Kate does not want to race Liz.
6. Is there space for all four pals?

"This was fun," said Kate, "but we should go before it gets too late."

"Shall we take this path back?" Dave asks Kate, Liz, and Tuck. "It can be one last thing we do on this trip. It will be fun."

"This path is like me, Dave," Kate said with a grin. "It twists this way and that, just as I do when I walk."

"I like this place, Dave," Liz tells him. "The red plant and the red rocks make it so pretty!"

"Can our pace be less fast?" asked Tuck. "This is not a big race, is it?"

"It is better to go at a safe pace with backpacks and things to take back to the truck with us," Liz adds.

The path twists up and back. Liz stops. Dave, Kate, and Tuck stop.

"This is not right," Liz tells her pals. "That is the same red plant and the same red rocks. We are lost. We should check the map."

Dave gets his map, but it rips.

Kate is upset. "What will we do?" she asks. "We are lost. This path is like a maze. Who will help us?"

"I will!" Dave tells them. "I can fly over the path and help you get out."

Dave gives his backpack and hat to Liz and Tuck. Then he began to fly up over the path. He led his pals back to the pickup truck.

"I can see it!" Tuck yelled. "We made it! This was our best trip yet."

What If?

Reread the four stories.
Then answer the questions.

1. What if Dave was not a duck? How might **On the Path Back** be different?

2. What if the characters went skiing instead of camping? How might the stories be different?

Share your answers with a group.

Get Started

Meet Phil and his neighbor, Miss Rose. They are friends. Here are some fun facts about them.

Phil	Miss Rose
• likes Miss Rose	• likes Phil
• likes to draw	• likes to have fun
• likes cats	• has a cat

What will Phil and Miss Rose do together? How will they help one another? Read to find out!

Phil

Miss Rose

Phil and Miss Rose

by Gari Fairweather
illustrated by Charles Lehman

Phil goes to see Miss Rose when he gets off the bus. Miss Rose helps Phil's mom. Phil goes to Miss Rose's house before his mom gets home from work. Phil likes Miss Rose. She is such fun!

Phil and Miss Rose play games. They tell jokes and make snacks. They make kites and fly them.

Phil and Miss Rose do so much every day. Phil likes to go to Miss Rose's home.

Miss Rose can jump rope. She shows Phil how to do it.

Phil jumps seven times and then he jumps eight times. The next day, Phil jumps even more times! Now Phil can jump rope just like Miss Rose!

Miss Rose can skip stones. She shows Phil how to do it. This stone skips seven times! They skip more stones and then hike back home.

Phil has fun with Miss Rose. No day with her is the same as the last.

Miss Rose and Phil ride bikes on nice days. Miss Rose takes her cat, Hope, with them. Hope even has a hat! Hope likes to bat at it.

They stop at a big stump. Phil can carry Hope back to the bikes.

When Mom gets home, Phil goes home, too. He waves to Miss Rose. Miss Rose waves back.

Phil smiles as he thinks about what he and Miss Rose will do next time. He bets it will be a blast!

Picture Hunt

Which words in the box name pictures in the story?

bike	globe	rope	pond
stone	phone	kite	home
Hope	vine	lime	roses

How many pictures can you find? Make a list.

Compare lists with a partner. Did you find the same things?

Blend and Read

1.	bite	note	bone	kite	cone
2.	broke	bike	spoke	smile	poke
3.	cent	come	gave	she	go
4.	dives	poses	slope	alone	shine

5. Phil's stone skips eight times.

6. Hope goes on Miss Rose's bike.

Phil Can Help

by Gari Fairweather
illustrated by Charles Lehman

Phil likes to draw. He draws Miss Rose and Hope. "Mom," he asks, "may I show it to Miss Rose?"

"Let me check with her," Mom tells him as she phones Miss Rose. Mom lets Phil know she is outside.

Miss Rose smiles as she steps in. "This is Hope and me! You draw well, Phil. Can you dig well, too?"

Phil laughs and asks why. Just then, Phil's dad comes home and gives Phil and his mom a big hug.

"I have a big job for Phil," Miss Rose tells his mom and dad. "He will like it. It has mud," she adds.

Miss Rose has eight plants to plant. Phil helps carry them. Then he digs eight holes for them.

Phil helps pick up when he and Miss Rose are done. He finds Hope in the shed next to a big pot.

"This is no place for you to hide, Hope," he said. "Let me get you inside and into bed."

Phil picks up Hope and sets her on her bed. Then he goes to sit with Miss Rose.

"You did a fine job, Phil," Miss Rose tells him. "It looks quite nice."

"I am glad you like it," he tells her.

Then Phil tells Miss Rose that Hope hid in the shed and that he had to carry her inside.

"That is odd," said Miss Rose.

"Will she be all right?" asked Phil.

"I think so. I hope so," she said.

What Is the Word?

Use the clues to find words in the story.

Clue 1: Phil digs eight of these.
Clue 2: rhymes with **poles**
What is the word?

Clue 1: Miss Rose does this if she is glad.
Clue 2: rhymes with **piles**
What is the word?

Now you do it! Give two clues about a story word. Can a partner find the word?

Story Captions

Read these words to a partner.

carry	ride	draw	eight
even	goes	may	those
seven	five	shows	white

Write about the picture. Use some words from the box. Share your work with a friend.

1. Phil can **draw** ____.

2. Phil **shows** ____.

3. Hope **goes** ____ with Miss Rose.

Lost Cat

by Gari Fairweather
illustrated by Charles Lehman

Miss Rose is upset. She calls Mom on the phone. "I cannot find Hope. She is lost. Can you help me find her?"

"That is a shame!" Mom tells her. "We will help in any way we can."

Mom, Dad, and Phil do a lot to help Miss Rose. They hunt up and down, but still no Hope. Miss Rose, Phil, Mom, and Dad are all sad, but they will not give up.

"Where did she go?" asks Phil.

At home, Phil tells his mom and dad about his plan to help Miss Rose. He draws Hope and writes **Lost Cat.**

He shows Mom and Dad. They will walk the block with him to ask about Hope.

Phil goes to homes on the block. He knocks and asks, "Did you see this cat?" He knocks and knocks, but he has no luck.

Phil does not know what to do. He wants to help Miss Rose.

On the way back home, they stop off at Miss Rose's. Miss Rose hugs Phil and tells him she likes what he wrote. "That was so nice, Phil!"

Then she adds, "Hope likes to hide. She may even be close."

"That is it! Hope likes to hide!" Phil yells. He smiles at Miss Rose. "I know where she may be, Miss Rose!" Then Phil runs as fast as he can back to the shed.

Retell a Story

Choose one story to retell to a partner. Use a chart like this as you plan. Tell what happens first, next, and last.

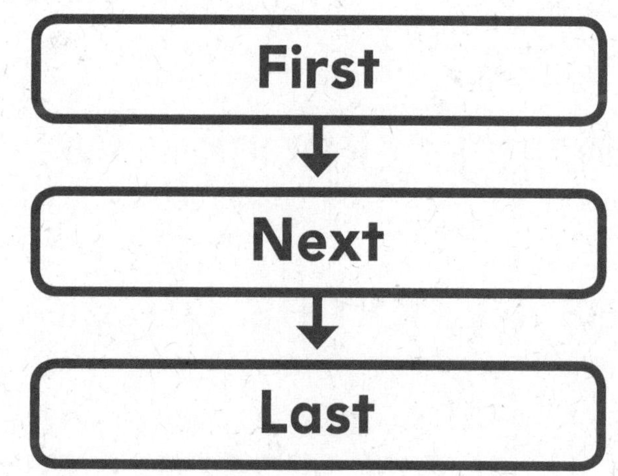

Blend and Read

1.	knot	glide	nose	know	wrap
2.	ride	role	rose	wrist	write
3.	thick	with	which	when	then
4.	knob	wring	knack	wrong	wreck

5. Phil goes to homes on his block.

6. Does Phil know where Hope is?

The Best Gift

by Gari Fairweather
illustrated by Charles Lehman

Phil runs to the shed. "Miss Rose!" he calls, "Hope is in here, but I found seven cats! Hope has kits! Hope plus six kits is seven!"

"So that is why Hope wanted to hide," he adds. "Now I get it!"

Phil and Miss Rose smile wide. "Hope had kits!" Phil yells. Phil sees Hope carry every kit inside and set it on the rug.

"Hope is the best mom cat!" Phil tells his mom, dad, and Miss Rose.

Time goes by. Phil and Miss Rose see the kits get big. Phil likes to help Miss Rose with Hope and her kits.

Miss Rose has a plan that she tells to Mom. Mom likes the plan.

Miss Rose gets a box. She pokes holes in it and wraps it up. She writes **Phil** on the box.

Phil does not know about Miss Rose's plan. Miss Rose thinks he will like it.

Miss Rose picks up the box and goes to Phil's home. Tap, tap, tap! Miss Rose knocks at Phil's house.

"Hi, Miss Rose," Phil said.

"Hi, Phil," said Miss Rose. "I have something for you in this box."

Phil gazes into the box. It is a cat that looks just like Hope! It is his!

He hugs Miss Rose and tells her, "I will name this cat Rose. This cat is the best gift! Now you and I will have black and white cats!"

Show What You Know

Reread the four stories to answer these questions.

1. How does Phil help Miss Rose in the stories? In which story do you think Phil gives Miss Rose the most help? Why?

2. Why do you think Miss Rose gives Phil a gift? What makes the gift so special?

Talk about the stories with a partner.

MODULE 5 ■ WEEK 1

* = *High-Frequency Word*

BOOK 1 Red Hen Skit p. 5

■ Decodable Words

TARGET SKILL: *Initial Blends with l*

claps, class, cluck, clucks, flap, flat, glad, Glen, plan*, plot

PREVIOUSLY TAUGHT SKILLS

Ann, as*, big*, but*, Cal, can*, cat, check, dads, dog, fun*, get*, hen, hiss, hisses, hit, hush, in*, is*, it*, jobs, kids, let*, Liz, lots*, Meg, miss*, moms, Nell, not*, on*, passes*, red*, Ron, rug, set*, sets*, sit*, skit, stack, stun, tan, tells*, that*, them*, then*, thick, up*, us*, well*, went*, when*, will*, with*, yaps, yes*, yip, yips

■ High-Frequency Words

NEW

around, come, other, people, work, worked

PREVIOUSLY TAUGHT

a, and, be, call, do, for, good, he, I, like, make, of, our, play, said, see, she, the, they, to, we, you

BOOK 2 Bags, Blocks, and Rugs p. 13

■ Decodable Words

TARGET SKILL: *Initial Blends with l*

black, blobs, blocks, claps, clips, cloth, flaps, flops, fluff, glasses, Glen, slips, slits

PREVIOUSLY TAUGHT SKILLS

adds, Ann, as*, back*, bag, bags, bed*, big*, bin, bits, box, boxes, can*, cat, cuts*, dabs, dog, dresses, fit, fix, gets*, has*, hen, his*, in*, is*, it*, Liz, miss*, nap, Nell, off*, on*, red*, Ron, rugs, set*, sit*, sits*, spots, stacks, sticks, tan, that*, them*, then*, thick, this*, top, up*, will*

■ High-Frequency Words

NEW

found, two, work, works

PREVIOUSLY TAUGHT

a, and, calls, for, have, her, her, I, like, make, of, puts, said, she, started, the, to, too

MODULE 5 ■ WEEK 1

* = *High-Frequency Word*

BOOK 3 Skit Jobs p. 21

■ **Decodable Words**

TARGET SKILLS: *Initial Blends with* l; *Review* st, sl, fl, cl

clap, claps, class, glad, plot, plum, plums, slip, stack, stick

PREVIOUSLY TAUGHT SKILLS

adds, am*, as*, at*, bags, beg, begs, big*, but*, Cal, can*, cat, catch, cats, dog, dogs, fun*, get*, had*, has*, hen, hens, him*, in*, is*, it*, jam, jazz, jot, kids, let*, mad, Meg, miss*, not*, on*, passes*, pick*, red*, rock*, rocks*, rug, sad, sets*, sit*, skit, such*, tan, tell*, tells*, that*, them*, then*, this*, up*, us*, when*, will*, with*, yes*

■ **High-Frequency Words**

NEW

around, found, other, work, worked

PREVIOUSLY TAUGHT

about, and, be, down, for, good, have, her, I, like, me, said, say, the, to, write

BOOK 4 Skit Day p. 29

■ **Decodable Words**

TARGET SKILLS: *Initial Blends with* l; *Review* st, sl, fl, cl

block, clap, class, classes, click, cluck, clucks, flaps, flash, glad, glasses, Glen, plum, plums, stack, step, sticks, still*

PREVIOUSLY TAUGHT SKILLS

am*, Ann, back*, bed*, big*, box, but*, cat, chats, checks, dads, did*, dog, fell*, got*, has*, hen, his*, hisses, hit, hush, in*, is*, it*, jam, jobs, kids, let*, Liz, miss*, Nell, nods, not*, off*, on*, passes*, pick*, quick, red*, rug, rugs, sat*, set*, sit*, skill, skit, such*, tan, tells*, that*, them*, thick, this*, up*, us*, will*, with*, yells, yips

■ **High-Frequency Words**

NEW

came, come, people, two, work

PREVIOUSLY TAUGHT

a, and, before, day, for, good, have, her, I, likes, make, me, my, said, she, starts, the, their, to, who, you

MODULE 5 ■ WEEK 2

** = High-Frequency Word*

BOOK 1 Red, Red, Red p. 37

■ Decodable Words

TARGET SKILL: *Initial Blends with* r

cracks, drop, drops, frogs, grab, grass, grubs

PREVIOUSLY TAUGHT SKILLS

as*, bags, bats, big*, bits, bugs, but*, can*, chat, cliffs, den, dens, dig, digs, dim, fat*, flap, flocks, flop, fun*, gaps, get*, gets*, hills, hop, if*, in*, is*, it*, its*, kick, kids, less, logs, nap, naps, not*, nuts, off*, on*, patches, pick*, plan*, quack, red*, rips, rocks*, rugs, sip, slugs, snack, snacks, snaps, spot, stems, stop*, stuff, such*, that*, them*, then*, thick, thin, this*, toss, trip, up*, well*, wet, when*, will*, zip

■ High-Frequency Words

NEW

again, away, because, cold, fall, full, or, pretty

PREVIOUSLY TAUGHT

a, all, and, are, do, down, eat, find, fly, like, live, make, makes, of, one, see, some, the, they, to, what, where, you

BOOK 2 Big Crops p. 45

■ Decodable Words

TARGET SKILL: *Initial Blends with* r

brims, crop, crops, drop, drops, truck, trucks

PREVIOUSLY TAUGHT SKILLS

as*, big*, bins, boxes, can*, chops, cut, fill, fit, fun*, get*, gets*, hills, his*, hot*, hug, in*, is*, it*, job, kids, let*, lots*, lug, lugs, man*, mom, much*, off*, on*, pans, patch, pick*, picks*, pop, red*, rich, run*, shop*, shops*, snacks, stack, stacks, stem, tell*, them*, then*, this*, up*, well*, will*, wins, with*, yum, zip

■ High-Frequency Words

NEW

away, fall, full

PREVIOUSLY TAUGHT

a, and, go, he, make, makes, of, other, people, she, so, take, the, their, they, to, too, what, you

* = *High-Frequency Word*

BOOK 3 Fetch, Dash, Dig p. 53

■ Decodable Words

TARGET SKILLS: *Initial Blends with* r; *Compound Words*
cannot*, crack, drop, fresh, grab, grass, grip, grubs, sunset, trick, trot, uphill, upset

PREVIOUSLY TAUGHT SKILLS
am*, as*, at*, bad*, bed*, big*, buds, bugs, but*, can*, catch, chip, dash, dig, eggs, fetch, fox, get*, hid, hop, in*, is*, it*, job, much*, nip, not*, nuts, off*, on*, pal, pat, patch, pick*, pits, plan*, plop, pops, quick, red*, run*, shall*, shell, shells, sit*, smell, snack, snip, spot, stash, still*, such*, tan, that*, them*, then*, thick, this*, tuck, up*, well*, when*, will*, with*, yum

■ High-Frequency Words

NEW
again, because, cold, fall, or

PREVIOUSLY TAUGHT
a, and, I, me, my, others, the, their, there, to

BOOK 4 Red, Red Sunset p. 61

■ Decodable Words

TARGET SKILLS: *Initial Blends with* r; *Compound Words*
bobcat, downhill, Fred, grabs, grins, hilltop, pickup, snapshots, sunset, trip, truck, uphill, zigzag

PREVIOUSLY TAUGHT SKILLS
as*, back*, big*, black, can*, catch, chugs, claps, click, cliffs, ditches, fetches, flaps, flashes, flat, fun*, get*, gets*, has*, hat, him*, his*, hop, hops, hugs, in*, is*, it*, log, mats, mom, mud, on*, pass*, path, picks*, putt, quick, red*, rock*, rocks*, runs*, sets*, shots, sits*, spots, stops*, sun*, tells*, that*, then*, up*, well*, with*, yells, yes*

■ High-Frequency Words

NEW
because, cold, pretty

PREVIOUSLY TAUGHT
a, and, be, calls, go, good, he, out, see, she, starts, the, to, was, we

MODULE 5 ■ WEEK 3

* = *High-Frequency Word*

BOOK 1 Class Six p. 69

■ Decodable Words

TARGET SKILL: *Final Blends*

and*, asks*, bond, desks, grand*, help*, jump*, just*, left*, lunch, went*

PREVIOUSLY TAUGHT SKILLS

adds, as*, at*, backpacks, bell, bit, boxes, buses, but*, can*, Cass, class, cracks, dads, did*, Fran, frog, fun*, glum, got*, grin, grins, has*, hop, in*, is*, it*, Ken, kids, miss*, mom, moms, not*, on*, pick*, plans*, sit*, six, spots, steps, still*, tells*, them*, then*, this*, up*, upset*, us*, will*, with*

■ High-Frequency Words

NEW

done, laugh, teacher

PREVIOUSLY TAUGHT

a, about, be, day, days, for, from, go, have, he, her, into, like, makes, many, or, others, some, the, their, they, to, today, two, what, work, you

BOOK 2 Frogs in Class Six p. 77

■ Decodable Words

TARGET SKILL: *Final Blends*

and*, asks*, bends, best*, bond, chants, damp, jumps*, land*, lands*, must*, next*, plant*, plants*, pond, ponds, rests, stands

PREVIOUSLY TAUGHT SKILLS

back*, bag, bags, big*, bit, bug, bugs, but*, can*, Cass, catch, clap, class, dads, did*, Fran, frog, frogs, fun*, grins, had*, has*, his*, hop, hops, in*, is*, it*, Ken, kids, leg, logs, lots*, miss*, moms, much*, not*, on*, pick*, picks*, rug, sit*, six, spots, stop*, swim, tells*, that*, them*, then*, tosses, up*, well*, wet, when*, will*, wins, with*, yes*

■ High-Frequency Words

NEW

any, laughs, long, more, think

PREVIOUSLY TAUGHT

a, about, again, come, does, falls, first, he, her, I, like, live, look, of, one, or, play, she, take, the, their, they, to, you

MODULE 5 ■ WEEK 3

* = *High-Frequency Word*

BOOK 3 Crafts in Class Six p. 85

■ Decodable Words

TARGET SKILLS: *Final Blends; Inflection* -ed

added, and*, asked*, bond, craft, crafts, desk, hand*, held*, just*, prompted, stamped, went*, winked

PREVIOUSLY TAUGHT SKILLS

add, as*, at*, bell, big*, bits, box, but*, can*, Cass, cat, clap, class, cloth, did*, dog, felt*, fins, fish*, flash, flick, Fran, fun*, get*, gills, glum, got*, has*, him*, his*, hit, in*, is*, it*, Ken, kids, lets*, miss*, mom, much*, not*, off*, on*, pals, pick*, plan*, quick, red*, sack, six, skips, skit, slid, sock, socks, soft, spot, spots, sticks, stuck, stuff, sun*, that*, them*, then*, thin, this*, tricks, up*, us*, when*, with*, yes*

■ High-Frequency Words

NEW

any, done, laugh, long, more, pull, pulled, teacher, think

PREVIOUSLY TAUGHT

a, before, day, do, for, he, her, into, make, my, of, put, said, she, the, to, want, we, what, who, work, you

BOOK 4 Track in Class Six p. 93

■ Decodable Words

TARGET SKILLS: *Final Blends; Inflection* -ed

and*, best*, blast, bond, bumped, champ, chanted, fast*, fists, jump*, jumped*, just*, land*, last, next*, tossed

PREVIOUSLY TAUGHT SKILLS

am*, bet, big*, but*, can*, Cass, class, did*, Fran, fun*, get*, glad, got*, in*, is*, it*, Ken, kid, kids, miss*, not*, pal, pals, plan*, ran*, run*, set*, six, stick, such*, tells*, that*, then*, this*, toss, track, up*, well*, will*, win, wins, with*, won, yell

■ High-Frequency Words

NEW

laughed, long, teacher, think

PREVIOUSLY TAUGHT

a, be, day, do, down, first, for, good, he, I, one, other, our, said, she, the, to, today, two, what, who, you

MODULE 6 ■ WEEK 1

** = High-Frequency Word*

BOOK 1 House p. 101

■ Decodable Words

TARGET SKILL: *Long* e, i, o *(CV)*

be*, hi, so*, we*

PREVIOUSLY TAUGHT SKILLS

add, and*, as*, ask*, best*, big*, block, bricks, bugs, can*, chat, cliffs, dads, do*, drips, drops, dug, dust, fix, fun*, get*, glass, grandmoms, grandpops, grass, gusts, hills, hilltops, hot*, hut, in*, into*, is*, it*, jets, jobs, kids, logs, lot*, lots*, moms, mop, mud, next*, not*, odd, on*, pals, pests, pets, pick*, plants*, rent, rest, rocks*, sand, shut, sit*, stand, sticks, stop*, stuff, sun*, ten, tent, that*, them*, to*, top, trash, trip, up*, us*, well*, wet, will*, wind, winds, with*

■ High-Frequency Words

NEW

another, house, houses, over, own, water

PREVIOUSLY TAUGHT

a, around, cold, don't, eat, have, like, little, live, make, many, of, one, or, our, out, people, say, the, what, where, who

BOOK 2 Houses That Go Up p. 109

■ Decodable Words

TARGET SKILL: *Long* e, i, o *(CV)*

go*, so*, we*

PREVIOUSLY TAUGHT SKILLS

and*, at*, bathtubs, beds*, big*, blocks, can*, catch, chat, cliffs, cut*, do*, fend, fit, frogs, fun*, get*, grab, grand*, grass, had*, has*, help*, helped*, hills, hot*, in*, into*, is*, it*, its*, just*, kids, lamps, land*, lands*, lift, logs, lots*, lug, men*, not*, notches, off*, on*, onto, past, pests, plans*, plants*, rats, rob, rock*, runs*, slants, spots, stacked, stands, steps, sticks, stilt, stilts, sunset, that*, thatch, them*, then*, thick, this*, to*, top, up*, us*, wet, will*, with*

■ High-Frequency Words

NEW

another, gave, house, houses, over, water

PREVIOUSLY TAUGHT

a, are, down, like, live, look, made, make, of, one, people, play, see, some, the, they, way

MODULE 6 ■ WEEK 1

* = *High-Frequency Word*

BOOK 3 Grass, Mud, Logs, and Sod p. 117

■ Decodable Words

TARGET SKILLS: *Long* e, i, o *(CV); Possessives with* 's

be*, he*, house's, no*, so*, we*

PREVIOUSLY TAUGHT SKILLS

add, and*, big*, black, blocked, blocks, boxes, bricks, but*, can*, cannot*, cut*, dab, damp, do*, drab, get*, got*, grass, grids, had*, has*, help*, helps*, hill, him*, hot*, huts, in*, into*, is*, it*, kit, kits, lamps, land*, lands*, lash, lets*, lit, log, logs, man*, map, men*, mix, mud, next*, not*, on*, pack, past, plan*, plants*, press, prop, rock*, sand, sent, set*, sit*, snug, sod, spot, stack, stacked, sticks, sun*, that*, them*, thick, this*, tips, to*, top, tuck, tufts, up*, well*, wet, which*, wind, with*

■ High-Frequency Words

NEW

another, gave, house, houses, over, read (past tense), water, white

PREVIOUSLY TAUGHT

a, around, from, grow, grows, live, made, make, many, now, one, out, people, the, they, ways, you

BOOK 4 Houses That Can Go p. 125

■ Decodable Words

TARGET SKILLS: *Long* e, i, o *(CV); Possessives with* 's

be*, go*, hi, I*, so*, tent's

PREVIOUSLY TAUGHT SKILLS

and*, as*, backpacks, bathtub, beds*, big*, block, but*, camp, can*, cannot*, deck, dishes, do*, end, fast*, fit, flap, flock, flocks, fresh, fun*, get*, grass, has*, help*, hitch, hot*, huts, in*, is*, it*, job, land*, lands*, make*, mats, mop, much*, off*, on*, pack, paths, prop, quick, rest, rugs, sand, set*, sit*, slip, snug, spot, spots, sticks, stop*, sun*, tend, tent, tents, that*, them*, then*, thick, this*, tin, to*, trips, trucks, up*, vans, wax, when*, wind, winds, wish*, with*, yak, zip

■ High-Frequency Words

NEW

another, house, over, read (past tense), water, white

PREVIOUSLY TAUGHT

a, after, are, cold, down, for, goes, have, my, of, one, people, pretty, put, see, take, the, their, there, they, use, way, you, yourself

MODULE 6 ■ WEEK 2

* = *High-Frequency Word*

BOOK 1 Brave Kate p. 133

■ Decodable Words

TARGET SKILL: *Long* a *(VCe)*

ate*, brave, crane, Dave, flame, games, Kate, lake, make*, makes*, shake, shakes, stakes, take*, trade

PREVIOUSLY TAUGHT SKILLS

am*, and*, asked*, at*, back*, be*, bed*, best*, branches, but*, camp, check, cloth, do*, eggs, fish*, flat, fun*, gets*, go*, grits, he*, hit, hits, hot*, I*, in*, into*, is*, it*, its*, just*, left, Liz, me*, must*, not*, nuts, on*, pals, plan*, puffed, rods, rubs, sat*, set*, she*, shell, so*, spot, stamps, sticks, still*, stuff, such*, sunset, swish, tells*, tent, that*, them*, then*, this*, thump, to*, trip, trips, tuck, up*, upset, upsets, we*, went*, when*, will*, wind, yes*

■ High-Frequency Words

NEW

always, began, gives, shall, should, things

PREVIOUSLY TAUGHT

a, all, are, comes, down, eat, good, her, looked, my, others, our, out, play, said, the, they, what

BOOK 2 A Swim at Crane Lake p. 141

■ Decodable Words

TARGET SKILL: *Long* a *(VCe)*

crane, Dave, Kate, lake, take*, takes*, wade, wades

PREVIOUSLY TAUGHT SKILLS

and*, as*, asks*, at*, back*, bad*, be*, bend, best*, but*, can*, cannot*, do*, dock, end*, fish*, flat, fun*, get*, go*, grins, he*, help*, helped*, him*, hop, hot*, I*, if*, in*, into*, is*, it*, kick, Liz, map, me*, no*, nods, not*, off*, on*, onto, pals, plan*, pop, raft, rocks*, she*, so*, swim, tells*, that*, them*, then*, this*, tips, to*, tuck, up*, vest, we*, well*, will*, with*, yells

■ High-Frequency Words

NEW

always, began, better, gives, hurt, shall, should, thing

PREVIOUSLY TAUGHT

a, for, her, laugh, laughed, like, look, many, one, out, puts, said, see, the, use, was, what, you

MODULE 6 ■ WEEK 2

* = *High-Frequency Word*

BOOK 3 Race at the Skate Track p. 149

■ Decodable Words

TARGET SKILLS: *Long* a *(VCe); Soft* c

cents, Dave, Kate, make*, place*, race, safe, skate, skates, space

PREVIOUSLY TAUGHT SKILLS

am*, and*, as*, asked*, be*, best*, big*, bump, but*, can*, crack, do*, fast*, fell*, fun*, go*, got*, had*, he*, held*, help*, him*, his*, hit, hop, I*, if*, in*, is*, it*, Liz, lost, me*, mud, next*, no*, not*, off*, on*, pads, pals, rents, runs*, she*, spun, tells*, ten, than*, that*, them*, then*, this*, thump, to*, track, tuck, us*, we*, went*, will*, win, with*, yelled

■ High-Frequency Words

NEW

always, began, better, hurt, shall, should, thing, things

PREVIOUSLY TAUGHT

a, all, come, down, for, her, laughed, my, other, out, said, the, they, too, was, what

BOOK 4 On the Path Back p. 157

■ Decodable Words

TARGET SKILLS: *Long* a *(VCe); Soft* c

Dave, Kate, late, made*, make*, maze, pace, place*, race, safe, same*

PREVIOUSLY TAUGHT SKILLS

adds, and*, as*, asked*, asks*, at*, back*, backpack, backpacks, be*, best*, big*, but*, can*, check, do*, fast*, fun*, get*, gets*, go*, grin, hat, he*, help*, him*, his*, I*, is*, it*, just*, last, led, less, Liz, lost, map, me*, not*, on*, pals, path, pickup, plant*, red*, rips, rocks*, she*, so*, stop*, stops*, take*, tells*, that*, them*, then*, this*, to*, trip, truck, tuck, twists, up*, upset, us*, we*, when*, will*, with*, yelled, yet*

■ High-Frequency Words

NEW

began, better, gives, shall, should, thing, things

PREVIOUSLY TAUGHT

a, are, before, fly, her, like, one, our, out, over, pretty, right, said, see, the, too, walk, was, way, what, who, you

MODULE 6 ■ WEEK 3

* = *High-Frequency Word*

BOOK 1 Phil and Miss Rose p. 165

■ Decodable Words

TARGET SKILL: *Long* i, o *(VCe)*

bikes, hike, home*, hope, jokes, kites, like*, likes*, ride*, rope, rose, Rose's, smiles, stone, stones, time*, times*

PREVIOUSLY TAUGHT SKILLS

and*, as*, at*, back*, bat, be*, bets, big*, blast, bus, can*, cat, do*, fun*, games, gets*, go*, has*, hat, he*, helps*, his*, is*, it*, jump*, jumps*, just*, last, make*, miss*, mom, much*, next*, nice, no*, off*, on*, Phil, Phil's, same*, she*, skip, skips, snacks, so*, stop*, stump, such*, takes*, tell*, them*, then*, this*, to*, waves, when*, will*, with*

■ High-Frequency Words

NEW

carry, eight, even, goes, seven, shows

PREVIOUSLY TAUGHT

a, about, before, day, days, every, fly, from, her, house, how, more, now, play, see, the, they, thinks, too, what, work

BOOK 2 Phil Can Help p. 173

■ Decodable Words

TARGET SKILL: *Long* i, o *(VCe)*

fine, hide, holes, home*, hope, inside*, like*, likes*, nice, phones, quite, rose, smiles

PREVIOUSLY TAUGHT SKILLS

adds, am*, and*, as*, asked*, asks*, be*, bed*, big*, can*, check, dad, did*, dig, digs, get*, glad, had*, has*, he*, helps*, hid, him*, his*, hug, I*, in*, into*, is*, it*, job, just*, let*, lets*, me*, miss*, mom, mud, next*, no*, odd, on*, Phil, Phil's, pick*, picks*, plant*, plants*, pot, sets*, she*, shed, sit*, so*, steps, tells*, that*, them*, then*, this*, to*, up*, well*, when*, will*, with*

■ High-Frequency Words

NEW

carry, draw, draws, eight, goes, may, show

PREVIOUSLY TAUGHT

a, all, are, comes, done, finds, for, gives, have, her, know, laughs, looks, outside, right, said, the, think, too, why, you

MODULE 6 ■ WEEK 3

** = High-Frequency Word*

BOOK 3 Lost Cat p. 181

■ Decodable Words

TARGET SKILLS: *Long* i, o *(VCe); Silent Letters* (kn, wr)
close*, hide, home*, homes*, hope, knocks, likes*, nice, rose, Rose's, smiles

PREVIOUSLY TAUGHT SKILLS
adds, and*, as*, ask*, asks*, at*, back*, be*, block, but*, can*, cannot*, cat, dad, did*, do*, fast*, go*, has*, he*, help*, him*, his*, hugs, hunt, I*, in*, is*, it*, lost, lot*, luck, me*, miss*, mom, no*, not*, off*, on*, Phil, plan*, runs*, sad, she*, shed, so*, still*, stop*, tells*, that*, then*, this*, to*, up*, upset, we*, with*, yells

■ High-Frequency Words

NEW
draws, even, goes, may, shows

PREVIOUSLY TAUGHT
a, about, all, any, are, calls, does, down, find, give, her, know, see, the, they, walk, wants, was, way, what, where, you

BOOK 4 The Best Gift p. 189

■ Decodable Words

TARGET SKILLS: *Long* i, o *(VCe); Silent Letters* (kn, wr)
hide, holes, home*, hope, inside*, knocks, like*, likes*, pokes, rose, Rose's, smile, time*, white*, wide, wraps, writes*

PREVIOUSLY TAUGHT SKILLS
adds, and*, at*, best*, big*, black, box, but*, cat, cats, dad, gazes, get*, gets*, gift, had*, has*, he*, help*, hi, his*, hugs, I*, in*, into*, is*, it*, just*, kit, kits, miss*, mom, name*, not*, on*, Phil, Phil's, picks, plan*, plus, rug, runs*, set*, she*, shed, six, so*, tap, tells*, that*, this*, to*, up*, will*, yells

■ High-Frequency Words

NEW
carry, goes, seven

PREVIOUSLY TAUGHT
a, about, by, calls, does, every, for, found, have, her, here, house, know, looks, now, said, see, sees, something, the, thinks, wanted, why, you